Wings

of the

resplendent

The song of Jaya Deva

Andrew Quilliam Brewer

We do not walk through this life

Nor do we run or crawl

We only glide on wings Resplendent

While we dream

And float above the awesome

Aerial of the night winds that resound

Always below us in raptured glory

While we sleep

I Bow to My Guru

Jayat Gurudev Baba

Neem Karoli Maharaj

To Whom this book is gratefully
Dedicated

Jai Ram

First published by Ingram Spark

Ashville NC   2022

ISBN; 9780578381220

Wings of the Resplendent

We fall

Into a brightness   undiminished

Into a depth of light   unknown

It is the immensity   come down upon us

With flames we cannot see

It is a vastness   unimagined

It is a space   beyond the furthest reaches of the

mind

We are falling into a deep   beyond any we have

ever known

And it is fast upon us

And still we do not see

And yet we fall

Into blackness   into void

But first   we must be compressed

Like gold   into our finest filament of corporeal

being

And then   the very bottom of the blackest hole

Will open only   into light

And then   there will be only light

It is a brightness   that grows   with each mile we

fall

And we are all still falling

Until the brightness   becomes a song of love

And then we may hear it

Pound and tear and weep upon our heart

Until we break from sorrow

And from our deepest yearning   to be more

And still we fall

We fall until there is no more

And no one left at all

We fall until we turn   to light

And then   the measure of our being

Is only a brightness   in a vastness   beyond

measure

We burn with a flame of love

That can never be diminished

And will forever grow into brightness

And forever will we sing

Until the wind of God says

Sing no more

Now if you gaze into the brightness of a starry

starry night

Know

That it is yourself

A million   million years from now

And there is no end

Until the very end

And then

We will all begin to fall

Into that brightness   once again.

The wolves grow white

in these mountains

They howl   and hunt for dawn light

On silver paws

They linger   to smell the new formed earth

That forever   yearns   to be more

Icy whisps   roll up in billows

Bright and blooming   from the night

And the bare trees   shudder and blush

As the proud wind   wild and naked

Blows   where it will

Undefeated by man   or by any power

Save light

The Sun   is the One   who rises

And all must rise

Even the wind   bows down

It is the self- illumed One

That all men   seek to know

And do not know   they seek

And so the wolves   stay close and howl

So the moon may rise

But the men are quiet

And waiting to be warm

And still   they dream of light

And the icy wind

blows where it will

Take all the glad moments

Every small and insignificant one of them

Every smile

of a wind ferried foil   of vermillion crush

Emblazoned upon the autumn

The madness of a Creator

Gone wild with color

Each sweetness of a hopeful gaze

From the smallest creature

That beams up at you in perfect trust

Each soft touch and fleeting glance

Between a lovers moment

Without the moment   to unwind

Like a wind rose

Sailing on by   your hungry eye

The days pass the hours gather

Like dust upon the looking glass

Such a gathering of tiny bits

That makes a smile   glow rich

And reach   for a moment

Into the heart so deep

Take them all   and press them together

Into a wyvern quilt

Of remembered fire   and forgotten love

And you have a dragons day

Touched only by the tip of a brush

To give the line

And just the faintest signature of God

And there you have it

A masterpiece of a master

Who loves in minutes   only

The briefest kiss

And then the day unfurls   how it will

But take them all and sew each scrape

Into a bright blue fabric

And hang that tapestry of loves bewildering

glances

Upon your wall

And gaze upon it " when you are old and grey"

And remember well what you were given for a life

And be glad

For each small moment is a year in heaven

then let it fall away like a falling leaf

For it was your song

And you were there   to sing it

Glory be   glory be   glory be

To Papa

As I watch the Sun

Creep slowly across the wet and cold thatched

beauty

Of a wilderness   etched by ravens wing

And lofty talons   soaring past

I remember my father

And how he rode down

On the thunder plane from heaven

When I was five

The squadron would come in with a magnificent

glory

And we would yell out

"The corsairs are coming   the corsairs are

coming"

It was a sight   that baffled the mind

Like a raging buffalo of beauty and majesty

And sang

Of the victory of men who loved freedom

And I would run out on the wide open fields

To meet him

As he climbed slowly out of the beast

Still breathing fire and smoke

A dragon slayer   he was then

And he remained so   to his dying day

He battled through his life without a compromise

His honor   remained untarnished

His gentleness   to all living creatures was assured

He was a glory God man

And he bid me ride the wing of victory

That truth may still prevail

"never forget my son", he said

"Never forget the true

And it will carry you home again

When the war   is done

Never forget the true"

HAIKU

First snow

Tips the world

It is cold   and quiet

A thin flame of forgiveness

Floats

Just above my vision

Ahhh

The starry night

RILEY AND I

Riley and I

Have made a pact   between us

It is an old mans pact

As we are the oldest ones around

We have come to understand our situation

We sit together on separate chairs

We gaze out upon the world

Shimmering before us

Our eyes meet   we nod

We understand that we are both

Counting down on a very short list

The moments that are left to us   like this

Simple yet profound

Because of the eminence of great change

Although we contemplate our death   alone

Yet side by side   we sit

Savoring a long and colorful friendship

Between a man   and a cat

These are our thoughts

The thoughts of old men

Occasionally repentant

Hopefully over confident

Given to romanticizing the past

With apocalyptic visions of the future

We stand (or sit) proudly before you

Never defeated by death

Grateful to be alive

Ready to leap and even to dance

(maybe slowly) into the new day

We fear no change

We remember those we love

Very well

And that is our friendship pact

To never forget

THE FINAL POEM

This is all you ever need to know

All that you seem to be

Is slowly burning   into light

And all that you already are

Remains eternal   So relax

The hands of the clock are floating free

Within you

And yes   It is ok

To dance

It is a sweetness

It is a sweetness born from dust

Yet never dies

No common earth

It is the ruby dust

That stirs the wind

And flows like lava

Through the crystalline rivers

That wind through the radiant mournfulness

Of your eyes

It is the fire nectar   Burning through my heart

In jeweled sorrow

Only the golden moth

With diamond eyes

Can drink from this pool

It is my sorrows joy

And my joys sorrow

I sing, yet still I die

I burn yet still I sing

It is the song of rubies

Born from joy and blood

And ravished only   by light

The song of luminosity

It is the radiant soul   of Gods soul

We are growing so carefully

Within the fragile and delicate petals
of the rose

Blossoming within us

Warmed by every breath

Its form encrypted by love

It grows under our care

As we ourselves are grown

From the same seed

What mystery is this?
It is the soul of the Soul
We share

This is how eternity is won
True love   made real
Impassioned by love of Truth
Infused by joy
By light revealed

Thus dawns the day
Of non duality
Which needs no other

Whirling radiantly into the present

Ablaze in the luminosity   of Truth

Burning through all darkness

In the firmament of the heart

That light may grow

Into a brightness unimagined

Then shall we sing

The song of Luminosity

Red rue the rabbits

Red rue the rabbits

In the lemon silver wood

Ten tails be followed by an Eye

Down burls the river

Through the blackened willows murd

Nine tails be listening

For a sigh

Thistle wood be ringing

On a watermelon rind

And the Murly Burly birds

Be blackly roaring   "two passed by"

Now the geese be calling freedom
From the high Soar to the sea
Seven voices singing merry
In a summer oft the lee

"Ah well ah wind " the jade be
sages
To the mole beneath the brown
Now six have passed the autumn
Where the leaves are lying down

Green bells be wooding
On a winter sabled bow
And the five rabbits rankled
In the rabbit worried snow

Wild the ganderlings be furling
White across the spring
While eight eyes go leaping berries
Where the only swallow   sings
Far out   far out   the tide be
turning amethyst to wood
While deep within the Alders Well
Three lonely rabbits stood

"Now," says the owl root tenderly

To the twinkling of the night

"What shadow, Bimble,

Passed us by?"

Two felt the windy light

Red rue the rabbits

In the lemon silver wood

One tail be followed by an Eye

Down burls the river

Through the blackened willows murd

Nine tails be listening for a sigh

Unstoppable Beauty

It is an unstoppable beauty

That unfurls before us now

Amidst the ruin of poverty

And the slavery of all those who walk
outside

The wall

Three million souls we have imprisoned

In the dark place

Yet, this unstoppable beauty

Stands on top of this monstrous
betrayal

And drops Her leaves

The fall is coming

It is the end of many dark things

And yet we are still a free people

Free to love   and free to die

And always the beauty unfurls before
us

Undiminished and unabated

Its leaves of bright love, now faded
and falling

And then the colors astound and
refresh the spirit

For It is a song they sing

A song of the golden time
And there are many that remember this
song
For it is an ancient one

Sung around the camp fires of our
children
By good men   and good woman
And we began to remember how it felt
When the songs of the brave and the
true
Passed through us

Around a fire that allows only truth
To be sung to its children

"Do the right thing," it flickered
"Forgive when you can forgive
For it will clean your own heart."
Those fires were bright and hot
And full of a mystery waiting to be
shone.

Then we were the innocent ones
And now the winter is upon us
And it is "the winter of our discontent
"

Made glorious brightness

By this beauty unfurling before us
This unquenchable beauty

She roams now among us like a
naked wind

Unashamed and free
She brings the tinge of gold to all we
know   and see

flitting everywhere like snow

She will not stop this beauty
Nor will She be diminished
Not by any treachery of men

It is the Revenant awakened at the
end

And now the New beginning will
appear

All swathed in flames of luminosity

And now is freedom come back to the
children

Whose hearts are still pure

And to the rest

There will be an abatement

Of sorrow and of suffering

And a time to remember the good

For it is a time of unstoppable beauty

And She will prevail

For behold the sign upon the door

"They will not all sleep

But they will all be changed."

Let us now then remember to follow truth

"Lead where it will, come what may."

And behold this unstoppable beauty

Whose time is now

Arising within us and without us

And all around us

As the leaves are falling

So now we may sing those good old
songs

And remember the true

And if we must die now

Let us do it with a goodness given

And a smile remembered

And a tip of our hat to the brave and
the true

That we may stand with them at the
end of days

And behold at last this unstoppable
beauty

That stands unflinchingly before us
and

Calls to our hearts last glory

In a final song

That we may hear again the words

This world is so heart breakingly
built upon

The flames of sorrow

It is in the flames of sorrow that we
burn

To make us bright

And then we are carefully burnished

By despair

And Grief

And promised Joy

This is the Love that pours down now
upon us

This is the fire   in which we burn

That we may see through darkness
into light

It is a river of grief

That runs along the shores of Heaven

From this we emerge

Then gladly walk upon the shores of
truth

The lives of the saints are filled with
the love

That sorrow only brings

Make no mistake

To this waterless country

The waters will return   again

And turn all deepest sorrow   into
gold

This way does the Mother walk

This is the alchemy of grief

Reawakened into a castle of golden
light

So surely does She tread

The smallest worm is not afraid

So carefully   that all darkness

Falls a glimmering

Into the passion   of the light

Wha Baba say

The problem has never been darkness

It has always been light

Too much light

In order for the world to be there
must be darkness

In order for the soul to be   there
must be darkness

At the moment of Creation   there
must be darkness

Brahman never forgets

All thoughts and all thinkers

Are saved by Maya

And thrown into the void at the

moment of creation

Like hungry seeds   dreaming of

light

Desire is awakened in the seeds

When the dream comes to fruition

And the Eye of the Beholder   is born

Too much light, and the chaos turns

to fire

Too little and it turns to water

Just right and the mountains rise up

And the Rain has a home

And the Wind is awake

It is the balancing of the shadow
That is the job of the living

Every time you make love real
1008 stars are born
And in between the moving worlds
Time and destiny   will dance

So is dharma made strong
So is beauty born
So is truth revealed

And much light is released from the
dissolution of the dark

And by this   the heart is made
strong

What is it that reveals the light ?

It is the heart   of course

For it is that darkness itself   is only
light

Waiting to be born

When you see the darkness know this

It is only love   that is calling

Do what you will

Believe what you must

But it is only   love   that is calling

The Flight Deck

The flight deck is ready   the river
calls

The turkeys walk together then

One by one, in no order

But courage allows

They fly at last over the river

The Applegate River,

just because they can

I pause here and wonder

How is love   still real

And yet   it is

And deeper than it ever was

That is a profoundly clear

And beautiful understanding

Of how life actually is

Love grows deeper

So the heart can finally rest

Upon the hands of love   and find

peace

All life's purpose

Becomes revealed in a moment of true

peace

How simple is that

Li Po

Lost in purple haze
Carried off by winged men
The great work   disappears

Alas for glory

Yet in the heart again   it sounds
It cannot be silent   forever
For the mountain has remembered
And so the men do also
And in their many lives again

They sing the old songs

Once so carefully made

And inspiration returns

like the Black Swans

To a royal court

It is imprinted in the mesh

Of the fabric of reality

This return

You can depend upon it

Many beside the winged men

Await the turn

Of the new tide coming

A fresh smell moves through the air
The poets have returned from distant
travels
And the fires have been lit again

Let drink be not a barrier
To the good mans' song
Those who would hear let them listen
Those who would be seen, let them see

The poets have returned

And now the rains   will fall

And once again the world will be
revealed

To be made of water.

It is a straggling beauty

It is a straggling beauty of moss

And dawn lit flowers   that follows
me

Hoping for love   yearning for
light

Waiting   for the touch to know

The real is real

How can I hold back

When everyday   I disappear a little
more

The song of Jaya Deva

And that day will dawn

When the heart will not fail

And death will fall to ruin

And then will awaken the Sun

The Son   the golden one

Ablaze in the luminosity of the
knowledge of Truth

Burning through all darkness

In the firmament of the Heart

Thus dawns the day of non duality

Which needs no other

And ignorance at last will be resolved
into light

The pervader of all

The sustainer of all

Illuminating all   including itself

This One, that is the resplendent
victory of Truth

Is victory itself

Is One without second

And never will be diminished

And so remains in the eternal bliss

Of the Absolute Brahman

Forever   Jai Ram

Down the river

Down the river past the falls

The days go swiftly by

Many lights are dimming now

They have all grown old

My uncles and my friends   all dying

soon

Death is upon the day and I stand

strong

And undiminished   and still

Lo they pass and words are lost

As days are lost

Death brings a wordless moment

And then suddenly   it is over

I send a prayer to those that pass

That they may not fear to love again

It is never to late for love   I tell
them

And if they are wise   they listen

The Eye that within the lotus opens

Let us arise now and go out   and
gaze upon the moon
That we may see the face of truth
And come to remember soon
Ourselves   we have forgotten
By moon and moth light stirring
Like the wind
We are the lotus flower that dwells
asleep within
At the end of our lives
Long must we labor
To come at last to the moonlit   mirror

Of the mind we have embodied

To gaze with a great loneliness

And a fervent longing

To see ourselves revealed

Beyond the veils

In our last hours

We must find the gold   we are

And hold to that deep brightness

If we would cross the river of our

dying

We go alone into death

And yet we are never alone

There is always the One

Who dwells

Within the lotus of our heart

This is the One that now we face

Not the devil   and not the Lord

It is beyond all imagining

The power of that moment

It is beyond all suffering

And beyond all pain

Our way will be unique to us

And it will drop us to our knees

Make no mistake

We will be grateful and we will be
horrified

For their will be no appeal

For now, we will see

No longer through the glass darkly

We will stand at last

Revealed

It is an ancient truth

It is an ancient truth

Gold is everywhere

It settles even in the wounds

Of the dying and the dead

It settles on the lips

Of hidden and forbidden love

And even stinging nettles

Weep with gold

It is the one that truth is wrapped
around

Upholding all that is

It is gold

That is the invisible nature

Of the natural world

It is the Sun that sings

A song of golden light

That all may rise

And all may fall

Redeemed by the whispers of the
luminous

Into the dying of the night

When the fire burns

When the fire burns
The white runs to gold
And winter laughs
Deep in snow I wandered
And the Wind took the world
And the morning Sun
Captured every frozen flake
And I was lost again
In golden rain

And when

And when we awaken at last
The dream will be revealed
To be a dream
And we the dreamer
And oh   but what a dream it was

And we will pause to remember
Those moments that were true
Still shining within our hearts
Still blazing
With a glory undiminished

Never to be forgotten

And then we finally understand

That love is real

The joy and the sorrow of the dreamer

Are held within the glove of time

It is time that wakes us

It is time that set us free

It is time that breaks our heart

And time that finally heals us

And in the end

We return to the house where we were
born

And where it all began

Into grace

Into grace

This day again unfolds

Always on the edge

The unknown lingers

Will it push me over into ruin

Or will there be enough

To walk the narrow ledge

To home   again

Ice days   and many spirits

On the edge of light

Vague traceries from ancient lives

Growing bright with new desire

I pause, and hold the gold

Close to my heart

The true repels the dark

And its bewitching promise

Of ghosts who hunger for love

The gold remembers the real

And shines

And the dark is filled with light

And is no more

And who will weep

And who will weep for us
If we will not

Who will bring the earth heart
Closer to the flame
If we will not

Who will listen to the tears
That fall like jewels
Upon the singing Lilly
That floats upon the eye of God

Who will see the Blood Moon rise

And who will touch the wounds

That fester deep   within

What shall we do

With all this boundless love

How can we hide from those Eyes

Those Eyes that always find us

Through the veils of anger

And of joy

Let no man

Let no man close his heart to love

It is the soul of God

We are growing so carefully within us

And like ancient wounds

Push deeper than we know

Always deeper than we can endure

This is the golden thread

That shows the way

And it will bring us to the core

Past all grief

Past all thought

Past all care of dying

And always deeper than before

It is the nature of death

To break new ground

To chew through diamonds

If it must

It will always find the deep within

And deeper will it drive the stake of
love

Until there is nothing left to break

At all

It is rare

It is rare
When we can face our life
Full on

It is far to bright

So we diminish ourselves
And fade away from Sun
Into the land of silhouettes
And shadows

And with our dear

And rarest breath

We breath the air of darkness and
sleep

And yet if we open our eyes

It is only light we see

The bright will burn your wings   yes

It will burn your soul   yes

And it will not stop

Until you shine   like gold

This is all

This is all you ever need to know
All that you seem to be
Is always burning into light
And all that you already are
Remains eternal
So relax

The hands of the clock
Are floating free within you
And yes
It is ok   to dance

The dream

The dream appears

Because the dreamer is awake

So now it seems

The dreamer calls you

To remember

It is morning

It is morning in the garden of heaven

And the ladies are laughing with the

roses

When they sing

The fragrance of dawn   fills the world

With a gladness born of rubies

The birds are not shy

Their cries are bright and fearless

And full throated

And the wolves cannot stop their

howling

We who must weep

Are lost in their brightness

And for a moment   We join the

happy chorus

Love can do that

It breaks down the barriers between

worlds

And then   it breaks your heart

again

Haiku

White tails be done with shadows

And dark lands

Glimmering will come from

Laughter   in the morning

And a mouse

A very silly mouse

And if there is tea

Well   it will be

A perfect day   after all

The mind is just fine

With emptiness

Just takes getting used to

Really   even you can do it

Scarlett emerald girl

Lapis burned the ruby dust

And tore the eyes of God

Riddle me a man

Said they

A man to see this world

And so   see me

The scarlet emerald rang the bell

And the world breathed another breath

And then I remembered

How you loved the roses

And the bright new dawn

You filled your mind

You filled your heart

You filled the day   with blossoms

And the scent of God Rushed out

Upon the world

Disc golf   to Gerald and Steve and Bob

What is it to have a friend in the
wind

It is wild   and it is true

So many fine days

Glorious in their glimmering of Sun

From the king of all mountains

We strode out upon the day

Free men   our hearts were glad

Our spirits strong

With magical discs we called to the
spirit

Of the wind

Come out we sang

We challenge you to play upon the
day

With a gleeful heart

We move upon the mountain

With a prayerful song

Come out and play with the
warriors

Of the wind

And you will be inspired

To be more than wind

We bring a wonder rarely found

The ancient archer walks among us

With fiery eyes and he rejoices

As we dance upon the meadows

And move upon the stones

It is the Archers way to know the

true

To find the very center of the hearts

embrace

And so   we will call to you

again

Come out

That we may sail our souls song

Down the mountain with a furious
gladness

To ruin   or to heaven

It matters not to us

We leap   we die and then we fly

And this will be our song

Whisper me rainbow down

Ah whisper me rainbow down darlin

The wimble bell rings love

The dawn is soft Paulin

Ah whisper me rainbow down darlin

Whisper is soft love, and roundly

Roll it with wonder, like lemons

And rose petal heavens

Ah whisper me rainbow down darlin

Laugh it out light love, like snow

On the whistle of heather

And blue love, and gooseberry
weather

Ah   whisper me rainbow down
darlin

Sing it out fine love

Like strawberry oranges

And willows and beeches

And baskets of peaches

And blue finch and swallows

And raspberry hollows

Ah whisper me rainbow down darlin

The deep dells are dancing

The river is running

Past red clowns and cymbals

And you and I love, beneath the
blue wimble

While tambourines play

At the end of the rainbow

Will lay love and be

Oh just as free

As the tangerine dancer

Who lives in the sea

The terrible truth

There is only God

Say what you will

Do what you want

Not by wonders or enchantment

Can you change this or erase it

And even you are bound

Not by powers   or believing

Not by oracles or holy sacraments

You are bound

That you may at last Be unbound

Thunder comes

Thunder comes

And if we are wise   we listen

Lightening strikes

Beyond our listening

And if we are wise

Not beyond our watchfulness

Love comes

And if it is deep

It rarely comes but once

Joy rides the wave of courage

And sadness the wave of sleep

Ignorance

It is our ignorance only

That creates this tyranny of the soul

Not the evil that we see

Not the demon that we fear

It is our goodness only

That we flee so fearfully from

Lest we lose ourselves   in joy

There is juice

In the things of the world

They are glad to dance

If you make them sing

They will invariably smile

Even the stars do this

And there are all the facts you need

To trust and to be gentle

Anything more   is redundant

Fathers day 82

And the wings are glad again

And all Gods glory is alive

And the great wind blows the horn

That only Rolland knew

And his ghost summons us

What have we done to bring this life
to honor

And to burnish bright that glory

Have we gone on beyond that last line

In the desert sand we made

When we lived our very best

And died with a full heart knowing this

That line still stands

And the sirens in the sands of honor
call

To the unflinching heart

Go on beyond

These limits are the measure of your
love of truth

Go on beyond

I have seen the darkness

I have seen the darkness
From the realm of light

It is a small darkness
That we fear so greatly

It is hardly worth the trouble
Of a worry

But Allah is merciful
As they say

So even that small darkness

Will be revealed

To be a sea of light

When dawns the day of luminosity

To zavi

Still on the river

Still in the boat

I watch as those I love

Slowly or quickly fall into the water

And glide away

Now I can only remember them

And that clear water of a grateful mind

Grows murky as it ages

Soon a hand or a foot begins to drop
into the water

And drag along with the boat

Testing for light

Will I still speak I wonder

When I drop away from the boat

And drop away from the body

And now it seems

I am gone from your touch

And your memory of me is fading

I have now gone

Where you will soon go

What can I say to you now my son

From the other side

Strive on grasshopper   strive on

And I say it   with a smile

It is great to be a poet

It is great to be a poet
And see the words fade into light
And not be worried

Obscurity haunts the poets dream
And death grins wider
The closer he gets

And then the moment suddenly changes

And now, there is still a moment

But it is not like the last moment

Now we must face the new day

In this new moment

We savor and regret the past

For an eternity

And then we start again

And there is a new boat

A bigger and more sturdy boat

(we hope) this time

We pray our dream will be astounding

Even to us

We pray that we will be at last
inspired
To make a mark upon the mountain
This time
Before we lose our pencil

It is not light

It is not light
I see
It is only God

Now breath the air
For a moment consider

That your last breath
May have already passed
But you never noticed

I am that golden promise

Made once upon the sea

That lingers still in waves

That never died

It will not stop

Until the dream is made to be

At last fulfilled

It is as it must be

For after all

A promise is a promise

And a golden promise

Must be true

For it is truth

That supports the world

And helps the Sun

To rise

Hanuman

Hanuman chose the good a true

So he loved Ram

But in his heart deeper than truth

Was his love for Sita

She was his one true love

And He was hers

Was it forbidden love?

It was only deeper love

This kind of love

Is rarely ever seen or known

It is divine love

Tiger blossoms

Tiger blossoms fall into the rivers
mouth

The river is glad

The blossoms turn to lilac dawn and
flame

And all the creatures can see

Lord Krishna has come back

Jaya deva   Jaya Ram

Jai   Jai   Hanuman

Jai Ram

There is always a refuge

At the heart of things

The deeper you go the better

You may rest in the heart

And be refreshed

The deeper you go   the better

Let go of your mind

It will not help you here

Be willing to fall

And then to fly

The deeper you go the better

Eventually you will understand the
riddle

Why not   do it now

When you remove the mind

What remains

Emptiness

Bliss   Is the better word

Bliss   Is the refuge of the soul

In the beginning

There is only bliss

And then there was light

Then came the breath of light

And the wind refreshed the void

And moved by the geminating

Principle of space

Brought forth   Creation

Homelessness

Homelessness is a frost upon the eye

It is a forever no

It lingers always

Closer to the ruin of all we know

We pray

And then we fall

Never knowing where to land

Always the wind blows as we leap

Into the coming tide

And the wave grows higher

And the surge is stronger

We cannot find the ground

We float

Until we learn to fly

I am remembering

I am remembering autumn days

That lingered forever

And never truly ended

They still remain

Like seeds

That grow endlessly

In the garden of my soul

It is a forever garden

Don't you know

With a table and a chair

And a pot of tea

And a fragrance of many days

Spent lingering

In the mountain forests and the rivers

And the winding little brooks

And oh so many flowers In the moss

And the buzzing of bees

And the hallelujah songs

Of deeply colored birds

I go there often now

To savor my life

In very small sips

And I often wonder why

I ever left

Within each leaf

Within each leaf that falls

Oh so many songs of light

Now ended

What a time it was

Wild in the wind

Wild in the Sun

And light would flow

Through our hearts

And our soul would grow

Taller and winder and stronger

The universe would expand

In the wake of our songs

Our world was a dazzling

Dome of light and storm

Filled with a thousand stories

Carried on the wind

Filled with the love

Of the ecstasy of sound and light

And when I fall to earth

I am still singing

As the wind

Carefully caresses my form

But I am a leaf

So my job is done

I have seen the miracle

And I have sung it gladly

And now I pass into that other world

That no man owns

Where trees still reach for the Sun

And rivers run deep

It is a world that I already know

I am not afraid to fall

Into the wind

And to the Mother

I return   again

Go into the gold

That is the way
And there be born again

Cast down the ring of iron
You have worn to long
Into the fire
Fill the mold of truth
With love
And see
The sparkle comes from deep
And will never diminish

If the gold be pure

So will the way be known

If the gold be pure

So will the way be shown

It is forever revealed

To the good and the true

Seek the truth

Come what may

Lead where it will

Let this banner fly above you

Emblazoned by a monkey

A golden monkey

His name is Hanuman

127

To Gene

It is the leaping

We remember in our final days

Those great moments

Of our hearts resounding

And unbending purpose

To make the jump

Impossible

Even to conceive

Yet, there it was

And there we were

And setting all aside

We leaped

And we awoke alive

On the further side

Of that chasm

That lay so hauntingly

Before us

We did it anyway

And then

It was a vertical assault

Upon a glacier

That rose unbroken

By any mans mark

Or even the promise of a foot

And yet we moved upon it

Like a shadow

With a blazing heart

And then

It was a sea cliff

Always pounding pounding

To the rising and abounding

With the waves of death

Upon it always

Pounding with unbroken might

And still we leaped

And saw within

The sheer terror of that impossible
bound

A glimpse of joy unimaginable

A sound that only God can make

We made that day

Or when the white sails

Unfurled before us

Down from our hearts glimpse

Of the perfect storm

Of a wildness unmatched

By any most terrible wind

And lightening and pounding terror

We rose up the billows

Of our breasts

And sang out from the deeper sound

A freedom cry

To go beyond that day

Where death was king

We were the prince of dawn

We were the sun ablaze

In the darkest night

And so again

We made that sound

That only God can make

It was a yes

That leaped beyond

And we were in it

And above it

And below it and all around it

We were finally free

To be that yes unblinking

In the face of Gods' own leaping

And so again

We made that sound

That only God can make

And yet

We made it anyway

The light is low

And the Sun is rising soon

Where I am standing

The world is sound

And the oceans are rising

Bright stars

Are burning in my soul

And I am crying

It is the halleluiah song

That runs through

My heart Never ending

And I weep to hear

The sorrows of the world

Slide by before my hungry eyes

And then I see

The glory song trail

And I rejoice to know perfection

Rises out of sorrows river

Like a silver mist

And wild

And wild the ganderlings

Be furling light across the dawn

And true

Is the wind that always follows

And now

Unfurled will the billows be

Into a brightness

That enraptures the heart

By whiteness

And breaks like a wave upon the dark

And there

Purloined by blooming

Whirl the radiant eyed

Children of wonder

Who have cast their hearts

To the wild and the thunder

And their laughter fills the gale winds

That roam hither

And nets of rubies

Swing from their dancing hearts

That bring all joy

To the gardens of the Night Rose

That are glowing now with plunder

From the pirates of Truth and wonder

Who live by the edge of ruin

In the luminous caves

Where the pearl divers play

On the silver waves

At the end of day

And wild

The ganderlings be furling white

Until the meadows weep

And the Angels

Lay to dream

And to sleep

No more

In the buoyancy

In the buoyancy of truth

We rise up within our bubble

Into finer and finer dimensions

Until we reach our level of purity

And there we will remain

Until we can light the fires

That will burn away all

Illusion and delusion

And purify the heart

And then we will rise

Up once again

It is a reverence

Born of joy

And many years of sorrow

The two have become one

This is how God heals the heart

Never ending

As there is always something

To regret

And yet

It is always over shadowed

By the remembrance of love

And so the day unfolds

First there is shadow

Then there is light

Then there is shadow

And then there is light

This is the breath

Of the living God

Surprise   surprise

The song of Kali

Oh let us sing the song of Kali

Let us sing the song of Kali Ma

That we may burn and yearn

In flames of Scarlett blackness

That we may rise and fall

Into the emptiness and the passion

And the terror of the void

It is a journey

Into the farther reaches

It is a journey

Into the ravages of love

It is there

That we will find Her

Dancing to the bells

The silver bell of lightening

And of ruin

All must be given

All must fall away

Nothing can remain at all

If we would pass before Her

It is only the purest of the pure

Who walk these shores

When finally
We may see Her face
There is only bliss
And from her briefest kiss
Eternal bliss
How rare is that moment
It is very rare
It is the last face
We will ever want to see
She dances there
At the end of days

Waiting for us
That we may know at last
Eternity

Children's poem stories
From the hearts of little beasties

The moon was dark   1

Ebony dark

Ringed like Saturn

With a glow of light

The spirits grew bold

And came forth

To roam between the worlds

Mouse could see them

As they danced and fought

He could hear the worms

Complaining to the Mother
With their full hearted songs
Sometimes She would listen
And send the wind
To blow them to the mountains
And the trees would breath a sigh
And relief
Would rustle through their leaves
Like a spring blessing
And mouse would dance a little jig
Very softly   of course
So as not to disturb the beautiful
worms

But just enough
To show a gladness
To the always radiant Mother

The beetle was happy   2
Rolling his dung balls
Up the hill
To his small home
He liked the work
Making dung into balls
Especially he liked
Rolling it away

Sometimes he worried

That his life was too repetitive

The same thing

Over and over and over

But then

He would stop

And listen to the song of life

All around him

He would have enjoyed

Being a song beetle

Instead of a dung beetle

But his mother would always say

There is no higher work

Than making balls from dung

Be happy

Doing the work

You were born to do

Your talent

Makes the Mother happy

And it is always good

To make the Mother happy

So the beetle

Just hummed to himself

And rolled his balls

Up the hill

The spider and the frog   3

  Walked together down the log

They had been friends for a very long

     time

There were no poets to tell their story

And who would ever believe it anyway

    If there were

   It mattered not to them

The spider would hunt for them both

And the frog would stand guard

  Over his dear old friend

And happily clean up the left overs

   And so it was

In a million years

They would be lovers

So deep was their bond

The frog would be a prince of thieves

And the spider

His beautiful and dangerous bride

And songs would be sung

And poems would be written

But their love would only

Grow brighter and deeper   and true

But who would ever believe it

Besides the small mouse

Who knew them both Very well

Run run squeaked the mouse   4

The snake is coming the snake is
coming

And he is hungry for love

Relax, said the Mulla

He will not eat you

Not today anyway

He only wants to hold you in his coils

And sing

Well , so you say said the mouse

So you say

But we all know

That you will say anything

When you have drunk enough wine

Not ever!   said the Mulla

Only slightly offended

When I drink the wine

I only speak the truth

Yes   yes   so you say

But how can I trust a drunken
Mulla

Well, said the Mulla

How can you not?

I am after all   a holy man

Throughout history, said the mouse

It is the holy men that have caused

All the trouble

And then

You blame it all   on God

Well, said the Mulla

Who else can you blame for
everything

5

The mouse was very careful

It was a full moon after all

The lotus pond was hungry for
reflection

And beauty   was in the air

It is the perfect soup To feed a
hungry mouse

Who is yearning to be seen

And full of love

6

(To Albert)

The Bear was old

But still very strong

With bears

True strength never leaves

He was no longer concerned

With the idiocy of the world around
him

For a moment

His spirit roused up

One of his family was in trouble

He stretched out a formidable paw

Filled with love   and invincibility

The freedom bell rang out

And all those he loved

Were very glad

To be loved

By such a Bear as he

7

The mouse was thinking

As he sat upon his favorite log

He was thinking about shadows

How they always pretended to be still

And yet the moment you turned your
back

They would leap and dance

And cause all manner of trouble

And yet

No one ever saw them, but mouse

He saw them

And they laughed at him

And did outrageous things

Just to provoke him

He complained about this

To his friend   the dung beetle

Who also only laughed at him

The spider and the frog

Were always to busy hunting

To be bothered

By his philosophical quandaries

It was only snake

That even paid the least attention

To this topic

Well of course, said the snake

The shadow world is actually more real

Than this world

If you can see the big picture

And I rely on the shadows

To help me hunt

They hide me in the shadow land

When I need to be invisible

And they show me where to look

When I am hunting

You are lucky

If they let you see them

It means you are a shadow watcher

And that is very rare!

Mouse felt rare and special for a
moment
But then he noticed
How the shadows laughed at him
And seemed to just ignore him
Most of the time

Then, he saw his own shadow watching
him
And smiling
So, he just smiled back
And then his shadow moved
Like he was dancing
And so mouse, copied him exactly

And moved like his shadows, shadow

And now his shadow laughed

And danced some more

Mouse suddenly understood

He was his shadows

Shadow dancer

And the door to the shadow land

Opened to him, And so

he decided to go and have a look

around

Red rue the rabbits

Red rue the rabbits

In the lemon silver wood

Ten tails be followed by an eye

Down burls the river

Through the blackened willows murd

Nine tails be listening   for a sigh

Thistle wood be ringing

On a watermelon rind

And the Murly burly birds

be blackly roaring

"two passed by"

Now the geese be calling freedom

From the high soar to the sea

Seven voices singing merry

In a summer   oft the lee

"ah well, ah wind" the jade besages

To the mole beneath the brown

Now six have passed the autumn

Where the leaves are lying down

Green bells be wooding

On a winter sabled bow

And the five rabbits runkled

In the rabbit worried snow

Wild the ganderlings be furling

White across the spring

While eight eyes go leaping berries

Where the only swallow sings

Far out   far out

The tide be turning amethyst to wood

While deep within the alders well

Three lonely rabbits stood

"now" says the owl root tenderly

To the twinkling of the night

"what shadow, bimble passed us by?"

Two felt the windy light

Red rue the rabbits

In the lemon silver wood

One tail be followed by an eye

Down burls the river

Through the blackened willows murd

Nine tails be listening

For a sigh

Curlews of the lazar dawn

Replumed the day
Bright and soft
And touched with fire

They flew on the invisible lines
To lift the plumage   high
To catch the wind   above

Where the brightest song was always
waiting

Poems of old

I remember

I remember the red razor sea

Who cast her children

Into the wind   and laughed

And we were there

Upon the ancient lava

We stood in sun and love

And watched the wind

Old stones remembered

How it used to be

When love was new

And blood was strong

And as we listened   the songs returned

Wave upon wave upon wave

They came

And as they sang

We sang

And as they wept

We wept

And we were glad

And full of tide   and very still

Rejoice in the day

Rejoice in the day

It is yourself   proclaimed

And never will it be again

And yet

Forever will the tide return

Endless is your name

But will you awake to see

Or sleep to dream

Each moment

Is a prayer to be made real

And only you   Can make it so

You are the One   The only
                One

This is your burden

This is your blessing

This be your burning song

A song of goodness

Goodness creeps out from under rocks

Bathed in blood and pain

It cannot be quenched

It cannot be stopped

All efforts are in vain

Do what you will

Say what you must

You will not change the core

The core is goodness

The core is love

It lies within you deep

You will not live
Until you find it
You will only sleep

Fishing with Jesus

My father moved gently
And deliberately upon the world
He practiced forgiveness
In ways astounding to behold

It is no surprise to me to learn

That he would go out with Jesus

And they would fish together

In the stream

That wild and glimmerous stream

With bright rocks and crystals
shinning

And deep water   flowing fast

My father loved to fish

And Jesus always loved the fisherman

It is not hard to imagine

The two of them together

My father fished the darks

For courage

And for the lightening strike

That comes from the mystery

Of the shadow

He knew that light grew there

Waiting to come out

And so he stood with Jesus

On the bank

And in the end

He grew to know

The power of the shadow land

To bring forth fish

That , by their very nature

Turn irresistibly to light
And so remake the hearts of men
Who fish for love

Fear not

Fear not the wings of poverty

For they will make you brave

They will make you strong

You will be cold and hungry for
awhile

But life will hold you up   Above he
falling snow

So you may glimpse the golden light

That falls always around you

Always   around you

And your heart will be glad

And stronger for the mystery

Of nothingness

And living on the edge of hope

And hopelessness

And always

The golden snow will fall

A song for my burning day

For the day of my burning

I wrote a song

That is what good men do

It is a song of gladness

It is a song that smiles

And from the depths it rises

To thank this world

My body was a good world

It never failed me

It took me to the mountain tops

And ocean deeps

It took me to the magic places

Where no man goes

It took me to the heart of darkness

And the depths of love

It burned me

And it carried me home

Thank you Lord

For giving me such a world

To shine within

I give it back to you now

May it grow a tree

In the cave of light

May it be a storm

In the forest of crystal men

May it live as a root

At the bottom of the Eke wells

And may it inspire

The hearts of men

Bless this body lord

It was good to me

Allah Ram   Allah who

Jai jai

Hanuman

It is a vast sea

It is a vast sea of consciousness

That emerges from the many crinkles

And the cracks upon the surface

Of the mirror of dawn

The One is cast into a million faces

Each is hungry and afraid

They smile when the sun is bright

And the day is warm

They run and fly when the winter

comes

Always searching for a better world

And then they die   and start again

Where will they go

And when will it end

It is only Time

That knows the way home

The first poem

The first poem came into being

With the death of a bird

Pierced through the heart

By an arrow

And now I see the hummingbird

Lost in the cold wet day

There is no food

There is only the cold cold wind

Surely he will die   Of loneliness

And I am pierced through the heart

Again

Haiku

From delusion

To delusion

Do I wander so

For thee

Never waking

long enough

To stay

In luminosity

As the fire bird mourns for sun

So do I yearn for light

My love is startled by pictures of a
life

Passed by unlived

And still it burns my golden eye

It burns for a remembrance

Of a time   outside of time

When I was witness to the fire of
God

And yet unburned and now at last I
burn

For my mother

You think

That because you have forgotten

Or lost your way

You have lost the day

Through dreams may pass

Love remains

Love endures

And even broken dreams

Will heal

Who dies when love dies?

Not love

Love never dies

Enlightenment

Seek the holy moment

It is that rare theatre

In which Truth stands revealed

Presence yourself

Into the holy moment

And thereby billowed out

By your own best hope and courage

Embrace and invite the present pulsing

And with your spirit then arousing

You unravel the many windings

Of the sail

Behind which the sailor breathes

And dwells and comes at last a-living

Seek the holy moment

That realm where in surrender

Means the enemy is yourself

Revealed and redeemed and resurrected

From this sincere yearning

Now a kindled

Grace awakens

And the Truth becomes

Self-evident

And that which you are not

You are not

And that which you are

Stands revealed

And the dreamer awakens

And the legion of your forms

Flow into the lotus blossom

And you

Stainless and shining

Stand revealed

And the whisps fall away

Into the autumn winds

And you

Stainless and shining

Stand revealed

And the skins fall away

With all their sins

And you

Stainless and shining

Stand revealed

And redeemed and resurrected

To the One

That you are

New Beginnings

The Navarone

is lost in Sun

and Holy cliffs

Sublime is the water below

Engorged with azure blue

And pearls of purple light

This is where I sit

To watch for waves

In that other world

That no one owns

Li Po and I and Lao Tzu

We sit together sipping our tea

Sometimes wine

Occasionally we smoke

We laugh when the waves are big

And when they break

We study the foam

When the Sea is calm

We write

And sometimes we sing

We have all died many times

Sometimes We remember

When We were last together

Often We were drunk

But not so much now

Now We are watching the light

Always the light

As it falls upon the foam

Of the waves who break

With times blessing

And then they are sucked back

On their long journey to the distant
shore

For the briefest moment

The foam leaves a print

Like tea leaves at the bottom of a cup

All that will soon unfold

Is written there

Everything you need to know is there

It is a window through times door

And then it is gone

Another wave has come

And so   still breathing, like the
rolling of the waves

We watch our time slip away

Before the final wave returns

We are the wave watchers

We sing between the breaks

And then we die

Usually, but not always forgotten

Are we sad?

We are not sad

We are at peace with the world

That is always dissolving

And reappearing before us

We are deep in the Heart of the

ocean

We are poets

What more could we ask for?

The heart of the Ocean

Is a forever love

Unrequited

Unabashed

Un-abated

It is a poets   Dream

A Jubilation Of Crimson

Flashes out Gods eyes

Winking light and lust

A promise of loves ecstatic embrace

Before the hunger strikes the flame

And bursts all bounds of body

That we claim

It is only a moment   that we live

No longer than a Damsel fly forlorn

Or dawn fresh dew

Before the Sun awakens

Sing out   before you fade away

Sing out   all birds know this

The song will be remembered

Though you may not

Sing out   while wind is strong

For soon

You will be changed

Again and again and again

But for this precious moment now

All is never was

Be glad   and sing it loud

For life is jubilation enough

To Susanne

Sweet winter mornings

When I would water all plants

Within your enchanted green house

While you slept bathing in loves
blessing

May the pools in heaven be filled

With that silent love

And all the roses that we walked
among

May they hang above you

And fall like dew blossoms upon you

May all my prayers for you

Be transformed into a fragrance

Of laughter and musk and rose

blossom oil

Moving through the pools

On lotus petals of lavender

And round your scented wonderment

Let tigers roam and panthers dwell

and eagles roost

To show you how I love you still

Let Pan awaken in your world

And bring you my passionate

And purple red plumed winged

And never ending love

That you may bath now within

And remember

All the love that never was sung

Let it now be heard

So you may dance me once again

To the end of love.

The Tigers of God

Tigers

Roam through my heart

Freely and gladly

Do they do they wander here

I have made them a home

In the wilderness   within me

Often their fearless blood song

Fills me like a forgotten dream

Gladly remembered

We often walk together in the night

Their spirit is a triumph of the
warriors will   And the poets heart

I will always love them

And so they stay close

The jungle of my soul is a haven for
many

And I flow leaping like the Ganges

In my many rivers   To refresh the
magic

Music arises from this union with the
wild

And I have gladly become a fearless
Champion of the small

It is a land of Blue Volcanoes'

And passionate low simmering embrace

And very slowly   brick by brick

Using only tears to make them stick

I have built a refuge here

It is known as the House of the
Morning

And I will rise in the House of the
Morning   And herein will I abide

The wind will blow

The snow will fall

And Suns will turn to eyes

Yet will I rise

In the House of the Morning

And therein will I abide.

Haiku   for Susanne

And now it is forever
And then   it was undone
Before the drummer came to stay
I had forgotten how the bells had
rung
For you
And they never stopped
For me
Hallelujah

The evanescence

The evanescence of the sublime

Blooms slowly or all at once

Out of the darker wilderness

Wrought by light

Forged by love

It is the burning

In the hallowed ground

Out of the yearning lust for God

Let your heart

Contemplate this flower

Hold on for it is dear

Remember how brief is life
And how long the darkness
From which it is wrought

Never stop
Until you must
This lonely journey
It is rare
And it is good
Find the seed you are
And let it bloom from out the dust

Tears

From a single tear

A world can grow

From this seed

A world can be made anew

Stronger than the tallest oak

More subtle than a lotus

Born of flame and dew

It is a mystery   this magic

It is a living poem   made real

And carved in stone by love eternal

And it is never lost

Birthday poem   2021

The drums

The drums of winter

Pour down and roar like waves of
wolves

From oceans deepest moan

A blue and burning epiphany

Of blast and thunder

From this thunder   I was born

And hallelujah driven from the drums

Of deepest glory

From the drums of winter   drinking
light

First breaking light

hallelujah light

Dawn bright and gold

It is a bright that forever blooms

And roars   and blooms again reborn

And the Green man sings and yearns

And leaps upon the winters drum

To call for light   from dust and ruin

From mountain song and river

Flowing with a deeper gladness

And the Green man sings again

And the water covers all

And turns the dust   to living earth

Wherein this leaping seed

Will finally bloom   and die

And bloom again

From the mist

From the mist
I wander like a blind man
Seeking stars to guide me
Following the crystal river

I drag my stick along the bank
I can hear the roar of giant falls
I can smell the green day growing

My blood turns to fire
And for a brief moment

I can see the galaxy unfold

And then I am no more in mist

Now only stars

And I am bold   into the brightness

And then I understand

This small self   and the mist

are one

Now only the roar of falls

Will guide me

But to what end

I cannot see

Lady Yama

Lady Yama

Can only be a brightness undiminished

In the face of eternal sorrow

Otherwise She would eventually fall

Into a darkness forever

She is a brightness

That takes the breath   away

And sends the soul   into the light

Greater than any illusion will ever be

She is an unstoppable force of destiny
She is the moment of transformation
In a sea of illusion
She is the Alpha and the Omega
Of all physical creation

With infinite compassion
Does She walk into your heart
And stop the beat
And stop the breath
And open the door to light again

Remember well
All those you ever loved
Who died

It was death that kissed them last
And set them free
And it is death   that finally
Makes love real
And pounds the gold
Into the finest filament
Of purity
It can only be love
That makes us better

For its pounding

And if we say   yes

Than we are always

The wiser and the stronger for it

We are never diminished   by death

Unless we fall away from light and

never yield

If we say yes

We are always reborn from the ashes

We rise when the phoenix rises

We burn when She burns

But She never stays dead   for long

And at the end of every day
There is only awakening
Into the next

Let is not forget

And let us not forget
The Splendor
For it is born like the burning Sun
It is   and suddenly
All is   splendor
And splendor is   all

Everything changes

When the splendor is born
Words will fail you

Your mind will be only awe

It is an awesome birth

From horizon to horizon

The dawn light   turns to gold

And burns forever now

There is no going back

Once born

It moves across all time

On wings resplendent

With an awe struck drummer

He pounds the day
And overturns to night
To rejoice in the only dance
Upon the aurora

For bright it burns against the dark
In waves of twisted glory
It is large   this Splendor

It is very large

The Night Lily

As the Night Lily blooms

Under moon

So does the heart

When truth is born

Like a Sun   it rises

When the day of dusk

Has run away

And ignorance has fled   at last

Bright does is burn

In eyes new formed   from shadow

And bright does it remain

Though dark may return

With the moon

Glimmerous is the day of non duality

When it finally comes

And when it comes   it stays

Like a warm embrace

In a cold night

And the Sun   also rises

To burn away all darkness

That has remained in the heart

And the cinders are blown away

By the wind of God

And Hanuman

The Dawn

The Dawn has returned

And today,

I remembered the blossoming

And filled with new light

I stood by the ocean and watched

The river that flows always down to it

Now at journeys end

I remember the song of my life

And I watch as it flows

In jubilation with the river to the sea

Completion is a hallelujah song

That must be song

Down on one knee

With grace in the heart

And new eyes   to weep in the

morning

The smile in the dark

Despite the great darkness

Still a brightness grows

Unappointed by God

And certainly unexpected

It has found a foothold

Under the leaves in the deep cover

Where the special tears have fallen

The tears that make the Baba's weep

for joy

Almost the rarest tears in the world

A deeper gladness is beginning to stir

In the long dark

The darkness is worried

As well it should be

The smile in the dark that sparkles
bright

Is a demon slayer

Oh malama malama take heart

And do not despair

For that which you seek is not hidden

It is here

A wish maybe   but no fantasy

It is more real than your sadness

It is more real than your pain and

your sorrow

It is standing here

Like the mountain you are walking

upon

Seeking always the summit

And you are already walking upon it

The Sun is only waiting for you to
shine

And it will run from the shadows   in
response

If you are

Only bold enough   to be

Authors biography

Andrew Quilliam Brewer, also known
as Jaya Deva is a simple sadhu and
a poet

Who lives with his son and two very
large dogs

And a murderous cat, in the remote
mountains

Of Western North Carolina

Occasionally he is visited by the
ghosts of Li Po

Lao Tzu and Hafiz of Shiraz

And then of course there are all the
strange animals

And bugs that come for tea and
conversation

In his own words "He has become a
champion of the small"

He is of course, slightly mad

But, he emphatically proclaims

That whatever good he may have done
in this life

He credits entirely to his teachers

And whatever suffering he may have
caused

Is directly the result of his own
colossal ignorance and pride

He spent 20 years on the island of Maui in Hawaii

And he has never recovered from the beauty of his life and the beauty of his friends.

Epilogue

Having come at last to the end of my tale, I realized to my chagrin that I had omitted an important piece of bug prophecy. The prophets themselves were deeply annoyed by my oversight, but I assured them that I was saving their work for the most important part of the book, the epilogue. They were of course skeptical, being bugs, but I assured them that their work would be high lighted and that the epilogue was always the most important part of any bible. In their minds all books are

bibles so I just let it go. The first
prophecy is the work of

Larry Mo.

"My name is Larry Mo. I am a
stink bug, and according to you an
odoriferous and invasive species, a
blight upon the land, my names are
legion.

But I come to deliver a message to
you from your Mother, your real
Mother.

She has lost her patience with the
human race and so she is sending the

Wave. And we are talking big here, and very soon.

Which means that very soon most of you will be fish food. You will not of course believe me, because who am I , after all, but a silly bug, and a stink bug at that, but it is true, nevertheless, whether you believe me or not.

Personally, I have nothing to gain from your immanent demise. I am not a scavenger and I do not thrive in a watery world.

But, I do find it amusing that such a pompous and clever species like you would have so completely done themselves in by sheer greed and stupidity, and have only themselves to blame for a the mess.

Personally, I think it is fitting that your untimely end will be so undignified and so completely justified. On the other hand, I and my kind will be just fine. And thanks ,by the way for your concern and kind thoughts.

I and my people go back millions of years and we have changed nothing. You and your kind only go back a few hundred thousand or so , and you have changed everything.

So, are we sorry to see you go? WE are not. The sooner the better in my mind. The earth mother will recover after a while,

She always does. But I hope she has learned a valuable lesson this time. No more invasive species, no more humans.

I am sure I will be seeing many of you now, very soon. We have many human expatriates here in the bug world. Millionaire, billionaire types who are now bugs. And so much nicer now, then they were, and so much humbler. I can speak from personal experience. I am a better man now, then I ever was as a human.

Now, I love this world and I love the Mother, and she talks to me. So, I have become a messenger to the few humans that can actually listen. There are a few among you, but sadly way to few, and far to many Frito banditos who only pollute

and take, and give nothing back. So, may the Mother give to you now what you so richly deserve, and soon, I say, let it be soon.

And take all your bug sprays with you when you go. And I say it to you, with a smile. See you in the next life, maybe."

The next story comes from my old friend the Dung beetle

Allah Bantha Ezrahiem!!!! cried the beetle with great feeling. He was hoping to impress the spider, and by some miracle, he did.

The spider quickly pushed him from the web. "I will not drink the blood of zealots and fanatics" she cried, "be gone."

Now the beetle, much to his amazement, found himself free of the web, and he hurriedly ran away to live another day, hurray.

From that moment on, he became a reformed bug. He changed his name to Allah Bantha and sang prayers every morning to God. This was the humble beginnings of the famous beetle poet and reformist, Allah Bantha Ezraheim.

Now, the truth is, that the poor old dung beetle was never a zealot or fanatical in the least. He was very creative, and he loved his life dearly, but he never knew why those particular words just came rushing from his mouth, with such intensity.

"Perhaps," he mused, "he was saved by one of his past lives when he was fanatical and a zealot, hence the reason for his present life as a dung beetle."

When he was later born as a man again, he realized that every life has a purpose and a meaning. And when later, he won the Pulitzer prize for poetry, he understood his strange journey, a little better. And he never forgot his life as a dung beetle, and a zealot, and possibly even, once as a spider.

The End

Well, yes, I truly thought this was the end, but then this box of new poems just rose up and bit me on the toe. Sadly, I realized I could not end quite so abruptly . So with deepest apologies to the zealots of form and perfection, I bring these last few poems, wrinkled and worried to the table.

On Lines Of Goodness

On lines of goodness do we float upon
the day

And follow grace lines   into the
rising dawn

And there, on mortal coils of toroidal
sound

Do we entwine the light

To bring us past the dark

And then we dance   flashed out and
bright

With all our colors clean

And so the dawn breaks new

And brings us out of sorrow

Into joy

And so is hope reborn

Into the failing heart

That rises always in response to light

Though sorrow never ends

It is with trumpets blasting from the

eyes

That Dawn holds victory close

And never dies

And so with Sun and Sorrow both

The light breaks out

And rolls in like the tide upon the new
day

And covers all that had been dark

With light again

The Pillars of Creation

The pillars of creation
Loom always above

Like towers of galactic plasma

They cast of stars
Like fiery seeds into the mold of time
And wait for them to grow
Into the pure and glistening

God stuff

They were born to be

No darkness can defy them

Nor treachery defile

They are Gods deepest goodness

In the garden of creation

And blossoming will be happening

No matter how ruinous the day

And it will be grand to see

One blossoming

One blossoming
So many blossoms

Soon, they will all be pushing over the wall
Into to courtyard

The Mulla's
Will be madly sweeping them out the door

After all

What would happen to our souls
If we only walked on blossoms?
"See as the flame sees
Everything then
Will be inside the light"
The candle flutters in the wind
And fears the dark
The flame sees no dark
It only fills the dark
with light

From the Wild Mist

From the wild mist
The wilderness arises
The deep calls me back
And the ocean   churns
The sea the sea   the sea

And the rolling breakers
Blast upon the day
And salty cliffs scream
Glory be   Glory be

And foam, bright and full

They blast down the rocks
And then   all lies in ruin
From the thrusting madness
As the waves draw back-
And let the seagulls pick the bones
Of the battered and the bruised

And the whales move like mountains
Through the fury
In perfect calm
And glorious equanimity

At the ridge line

Here   At the ridge line

I can see the path

That leads over the mountains

Basho smiles   and picks up his
walking stick

It is always up now   it seems

Many bodies will fall away

From -this next ascent

But, all my friends also

Pick up their walking sticks and smile

They will follow me, once again

Even though our spirits only

May be walking this time

And the journey will be long

It is a fellowship that has endured

Many lifetimes   Why should it stop

now

The fun is just beginning

Tiger Meadows   to Susanne

It was a magical land

Of pure deep and fragrant grass

Tiny crystalline fairies

And streams that flowed deep and
hidden   Full of mint

And elegant madness

Dancing through the rills

That ran wild and bright

With tiny flowers   And horse tails

All a shimmering   in joy

We float upon the lilies

We float upon the lilies
Over deep water
The fragrance is full of goodness
Beneath the calm
Awaits the turbulent emergence of our
destiny
Always   unknown
Each moment is a crescendo of grace
Upon waves of jubilation and despair
But we float in a sea of Flowers
Surely that must count for something?

The birds are never worried

And God   is everywhere

And at the end

At the very end

There will always be

The Smile in the dark that sparkled
bright

In the goobly gook den

Where only weasels fight

Where things that never should be

Go glibly forth into the night

There lived a quantum lark

Of phantom green and shimmered light

Who dwelt within the other time

That all do know but have no sight

It was a rhyme of gladness

Left from ancient tales

That always were but soon forgot

By the children of the fragrant sails

Of happy pirates

Lost in the land of a thousand bells

More than a rhyme

And bigger by far than any spark

It shone from the deepest

And the darkest well

More than a glimmer

It left a mark that burned forever

With a luminous light

It was the Smile in the dark that
sparkled bright

It came from the heart of course

From the heart of all things

But invisible to most

It lingered in the deeper dark

Where children's fears would go

To wait for any who would dare

To venture past the deepest snow

And face that dreaded day

A reconning to fear but never know

And there at the bottom

Of that dreadful well

Lay the spark alive

And oh so well

And oh so bright

Never to be darkened

Never to be lost without light

It only grew brighter and brighter by
far

Than the biggest full glimmering

Ball of a star

It was brighter than all

That had ever been bounded by
darkness

And left to be sounded by whales

In the depth of the darkness

It was diamondized now

It was clearly a spark

Growing by fits and lazar fire bits

It was a glimmerous bright light

A moaning of diamonds and joyous
delight

It moved past all knowing

Into the fast of the flowing

And there in the center of sight

At the edge of the falls

Shone the Smile in the dark that
sparkled bright

Always it waited, always it knew

The invisible goodness

On tiny wet shoes

Would come looking for hope and for
light

And It would be there

Where no light would float

On the edge of all things that are real

It would be there

Where only was dark

And suddenly Lo

A Smile would appear

And then brightness would grow beyond
measure

And all things that live

In the fear and the dark

Would be suddenly banished

And run off the pier

And then all the good seeds

Of gladness and joy

Would be born once again without
madness

And any small feet

That were lingering there

Would be suddenly aloft on large
wings

And could see now quite clearly

Though filled with delight

The Smile in the dark that sparkled
bright.

The end of innocence

Purple roses

Blooming through the ice

On silver petals in the meadows

Where my tigers run and weep

Beauty that is beyond the crush

Of life's eternal push

To know God

A fragrant eternal kind of beauty

Like a kiss

Never forgotten

That precedes the death of glory

And redemption

It lives only in the truly wild

And the truly free

How rare is that

It is very rare

Whippoorwill wings will always
sing

and

Go easily into light
As do the tears of Babas

Proud stones stand tall

Wind will blow the rest to dust

Water covers all

Slowly we tread upon the day

And yet

A lifetime is gone but in a blink

Really what are we waiting for

Now is all

There ever is to do

Or be

Or seek to know

Blink twice   and start again

Perhaps this time

As a razzelberry

NOW This is the End

The final End   and a most glorious end indeed

maybe

Andrew Quilliam Brewer

Jaya Deva   C C 2022

Cover illustration by Joan Doyle

www.theartistryoflife.com

The flame trees   burned the
innocence   Deep in the jungle

You can hear the tigers moan

For love is brief   and bottomless

The Peruvian Shaman twirled his
passion beads

The dance had begun again

He stomped his feet   until they
bled   On sacred ground

And the rainbow passion birds

Flew all around

And the Flame trees sang a hallelujah
song

To call the bright and lusty dawn

I wish to gratefully, thank and acknowledge:

Joan Doyle

For her inspired cover illustration once again you stepped up when you were needed   thank you Joan

The vast and formidable labors of my uncle

Dr Don Dudley Bushnell

Without whose inspiration and persistence this book

Would never have been published thank you uncle

May the apple blossoms of divine
erudition

Always abound in your being

My son   Xavier Shivaya
Alexander Kanaio

For doing all the heavy lifting for
this book

To my beloved wife Susanne E
Still (C C Zongmo)

For her eternal love and her
boundless creative spirit

Standing on the other shore

Standing on the shore

Listening to the waves

That always and forever sing

Of God

The metaphor is simple

With grace

We rise above the wave

And so ride upon the turbulence

With a calm joy, under the sun

Otherwise , the inevitable law of the vortex

Will pull us down To be pounded

By that same turbulence

That now we ride upon

Unless it be struck

This bell will not ring

Its shape, proclaims its' song

But still it must be rung

To sing

And sing it must

Or fall to ruin

How many unstruck bells

Have fallen into rust ?

That is a sorrow   unfathomable

A song that was never heard

A bell that was never rung

That one who is born to ring the bells

Is a gift from God

And ring them he must

For the Sun only rises

From this song

We step out

We step out   like sunlight

Onto the vastness of time

And dance to the day and to the dawn

A prayer of gratitude emerges

Just so   we say

Just right

AH   YES   AH HA   AH HUM

ALWAYS and forever

On the winds of the Divine

Unfurls the sails

Of the dawn   rising

And then

We rise

Purple shadows

Purple shadows in delight

Are always first   but now

The fawns are restless

It glows and it grows

This stirring   you know

It never stops

It roves through the radium brightness

Looking for turquoise

And tears

But it never   stops

Blue jaguar

When I saw her first
She was grieving
Gazing out from a distance
Beyond all time
Glowing
Far and deep
Into the Nubian wilds
Perfect and bright and fierce   she was

And she will   be again

This is her way

She puts it on the scales of heaven
Like butter   for the Gods

Victory is her name
Though she may weep
Never will she be defeated

Not ever

This is the way of heaven
This is the way of truth
And so
She walks in black
Always by my side

Dancing into the light

Fiery into the dark

Flowing like a comet

Through the night

And then

The dawn

The stream

The stream

Of our whispers of past delights

Moves slowly By gravity

Into the river of our soul

It is a timeless fluttering of snap shots

That floats   like butterfly's

Just above the river

Outside the mind

And above the waves that move us along

It is the watercourse way

That we always return to

To remember ourselves And be free

The abergast

The abergast is done with time

No more that dripping clock be wound

No more it's face

Upon the mirror

Of eternity

Now   is enough

Creation still abides

Within the Nature

Of the Divine

And so it prevails

But now

The elegant moment is arising

And calls forth to the precious heart

Be here   Be still   Be now

And the heart

Is beginning to listen.

The quest

The hunt for excellence runs deep

Through the heart

That loves Truth

Truth is the gold that glitters

And makes the spirit   glad

Always compelling to the wise

Because only Truth   endures

The elegant moment

Is resplendently adorned

With excellence

It is woven into the fabric of Truth

The heart cries out for purity
And excellence always arises
Like the dew

Without excellence
The heart cannot finally rest
It is the still point
In the arc
Of a perfect cut
And the sword
Is always brighter for it
The mind is polished

By the hearts deep yearning

And Truth

Is set free

To shine

In the growing dark

Like a song

It rises   with the dawn

Vermillion dragon flies

Drink nectar

From my lips

As I rise from the deeper deep

Forgiveness flows

From my eyes

And I dance to the song

That can never be sung

And I let my jungle beasts   run

It is not without sorrow

That I walk here

It is not without regret

And deep sadness

But the waves of my ocean

Are fearless   and bright

And they come

Oh they come

And they break

With a crashing delight

Oh they break

With a crashing delight

From a single tear

A word can grow

From this seed

The world can be made   anew

Stronger then the tallest oak

More subtle than a lotus

Born of flame   and dew

It is a mystery   this magic

It is a living poem

Authors note

The truth dwells forever at the heart of all
creation

This is the poet's way

This is the poet's song

This is the eternal fellowship

That flows beyond

It is the final word

That will rise up

in the new dawn.

THE END   THE END

The final end

The glorious   and bug glorious

end

Andrew Quilliam Brewer
cc2022

Oooppps   almost

forgot

The quantum smile

We return always to where we began

Time is irrelevant

The journey is always across the sea

And up impossible waterfalls, and down
wild rivers

Only the very best

Will arrive back home

Sometimes, it is only the best

Of the best

When you add time back

Into the equation

Everything tends to balance out

And we and the salmon come together
as one

We are not going to   any where

We are only returning

And in the process

The universe has been created

The return

Is the process

That creates the universe

So now

"Wait a minute," you say

"You are saying that creation is
nothing personal?"

"Well," I say,

"It depends on how personal

Your own experience of your life has
been

It is always personal

But sadly often unappreciated and
ignored

It turns out

That the experience of Truth, in
whatever form

Is always personal

And I mean

Deeply , deeply personal

So if its personal you want

Seek the Truth

Lead where it will

Come what may"

Andrew Quilliam Brewer

NOW   THIS IS THE END

TRULY

Yes   do you see now?

300

The very end   indeed

Lightning Source UK Ltd.
Milton Keynes UK
UKHW020814010822
406672UK00010B/1012